Poetic Love Essentials

Tabitha Edwards-Walton

Energion Publications
Gonzalez, FL
2017

Cover Design: Tabitha Edwards-Walton & Henry Neufeld

Cover image credit: Adobe Stock, # 88966141 and 101955918

ISBN10: 1-63199-353-4
ISBN13: 978-1-63199-353-4

Energion Publications
P. O. Box 841
Gonzalez, FL 32560

energion.com
pubs@energion.com
850-525-3916

TABLE OF CONTENTS

Introduction

There are two very strong emotions that people tend to use as everyday words. Those emotions happen to be love and hate. As I write *Poetic Love Essentials*, I will only write about the emotions of love.

When I say people use these words every day. I mean people will say things like I love food, I love flowers, I hate when it rains or I love that song, I love you. I think by now you get the point I am trying to emphasize. However, people sometimes never really feel the emotion of love.

Love is a very deep emotion that is felt by the mind body and soul. It is and should be so powerful that it truly will move a person. Love can make a person euphorically happy. Love can make some feel the deepest sorrow. Love can make someone blind, speechless, and it can make someone as strong as an ox. Love is unconditional. Love sees no colors. Love does not judge. Love has no boundaries. If the true emotion is felt in love, it is very peaceful. This book will display poetry about love using the emotion of love and not just the saying of love. I will have attempted to use the art of my poetry to allow my reader to see the story, to be there in the scene, the reader will want to get a full image. The reader will feel the emotion of love.

An Endless Kind of Love

I would follow in your footsteps.
That is what falling in love has made me want to do.
I would not care if my legs got a million cramps.
I would walk across coals of red hot fire after you if I had to.

I would swim the open seas,
I would jump from the highest plane.
I would live in the forest with the wild animals in the trees.
I would endure the heat of the desert terrain.

I would run a hundred mile race.
I would get hit by a car.
I would take pepper spray to the face.
Your love would make me do things that sound bazaar.

I would make your life worthwhile.
I would give you purpose.
I would make you want to smile.
The love I will give to you in return would be endless.

Broken Road

He says to her,
Persuade me to stay.
I want us to be closer.
I want our love to grow stronger than yesterday.

He said, I feel like we have traveled down a broken road.
I don't like how that makes me feel.
The tension between us is about to explode.
I want our relationship to repair, and our hearts to heal.

He stated, I believe this relationship will take both of us.
I want to do my part.
How to start again is what we need to discuss.
Let us not wait another minute to start.

He looked to her and said, I know we are still strong.
It will just take some dedicated labor.
Together is where we belong.
I have devoted my life to you forever.

LOVE AND RELATIONSHIPS

Love is when one makes a deep emotional connection.
It is a bond that is felt from the heart.
It can be profound and soulful.
It is so powerful, it should never be questioned.

Love that is felt is different from person to person.
The love for a child is not the same as the love for a parent.
The love for your spouse may be deeper, more intimate.
The love in all relationships comes from the strength of the emotion.

If one has a relationship with another, there could be love.
One could love a friend. One could love a stranger.
Love should be unconditional and nonjudgmental.
Expressing love is something everyone should be proud of.

THE ONLY LOVE SHE HAS EVER KNOWN

The moment when first he came into view.
She said to herself, *Who is that boy?*
I wish I had a boyfriend like him.
I know he is the one I want to give all my heart to.

She always watched him from afar.
At the time he was dating another girl.
She often laid awake at night to observe the night sky.
So she could wish to be him if she saw a falling star.

When he ended his current relationship, it was to her surprise.
They soon started dating.
He looked to her and said, "I am glad we met!"
He had compassion and he had love in his eyes.

The next event that happened, she became his bride.
They made a wonderful family.
They spent many years together.
They made a life together.
Hand and Hand, Heart to Heart and Side by Side.

HE IS THE LIGHT OF MY LOVE

My soul is darkening.
The light inside is dimming.
My love is weakening.
It is harder to concentrate on listening.

The Beauty inside me is getting harder to see.
I feel the pressure of the burdens in my heart.
I know his presence is there.
I know he walks beside me.

I need to learn to be quiet and to be still.
I need to learn the act of forgiving.
I need to indulge in trust,
He will restore my light, my love and my will.

My Faith I need to replenish.
He is always my guide.
He will lead me back to the light inside.
His Heavenly grace will not deny me the Love I cherish.

Searching My One True Love

I am in search of that perfect person to surrender my love to.
After all we as humans are always trying to find our one and only mate.
I continue to look for the one that will complete this puzzle.
I know it will be love at first sight, not just anyone will do!

I have observed from high and low, without success.
I have been all over the land.
I have yet to find the one.
All the pieces have to fit just right, I will not settle for any less.

I have looked every place that I can think of.
Are our paths destined to cross?
I need us to meet!
Where is my one true love?

One day, I happen to pass by a mirror.
I heard a voice whisper,
"Hey you!"
It said, "Look inside, love and honor."

That day I realized I previously had been looking in the wrong direction.
Where I needed to be looking was from inside out.
I needed to take a long hard look at myself.
I need to ask myself some serious questions.

The voice I heard that day was my soul, it was calling my own bluff.
It wanted my heart to be heard.
It said, "Who are you kidding, you cannot love another.
Because you do not even love yourself enough."

These words were harsh to hear.
But I had to face the truth.
I had to respect and love myself.
I had to release my inner most fear.

The love that I was looking for, was hidden deep inside.
I realized I did not have to search anymore because,
I had finally found my true love.
Now I am happy and full of pride.

THE SMILE THAT CHANGED HIS HEART

She smiled at him.
He smiled back at her.
He lights up at the mention of her name,
His head and heart starts to swim.

She was his first love.
She sat by him in his class.
She would help him stay on task.
He still holds her high above.

THESE TWO HANDS

Within these two hands of mine
I promise to love you forever.
These two hands will hold yours
anytime you need them to.
These two hands will help you should you fall.
These two hands will embrace you during times of sorrow.
These two hands will write for you if you need them to.
These two hands will dress you
should the day come when you can no longer do that task.
These two hands will feed you.
These two hands will pray for you.
With these two hands I am making the symbol of a heart
to let you know how much I love you, Mom,
because I am not there to hug you
with these two hands.
Happy Mother's Day!

The Love Found on a Nature's Trail

This is the place I go to reflect,
Because I don't have to speak.
I sit quietly and watch the small animals
Play hide and seek.
They dart in and out around the trees,
One could truly fall in love with the sound of the birds,
On days like these.

The sun warming my face.
Off in the pastures,
the horses enjoy a nice little mid-morning race.
My ears are also tuned into a babbling creek.
This makes me want to stay here seven days a week.

My lungs are filled with the freshness of the air.
I could just sit on this bench,
Listening, watching, I sit and I just stare.
I feel so much love inside.
Out here I share with God the beauty of His pride.

BOOTS AND TAGS

He closed the door to the car.
He knew he had to do what his heart had called upon him to do.
His love for his country out weighed the thoughts of war.
He said to himself, Dad, I will be a soldier just like you.

He proudly walked into the recruiter's office wearing all smiles.
They issued him his first pair of boots and gave him his dog tags.
These two things have been with him for many of miles;
His boots have been through so much terrain they have been worn to rags.

He trained and he deployed.
He said he would come home one day.
Bombs, bullets and enemy fire he tried to avoid.
He just did not know it would be this way.

A mighty solider he was indeed.
He got caught in a line of enemy fire, they really let it rip.
He never showed fear, he knew he had to try to proceed.
Those boots and tags made one last trip.

Home, without the man inside.
When he was laid to rest,
Sadly, that brave soldier's family cried.
His son has his boots and tags inked on his chest.

I Have Loved You From Inside Out!

I did not have to see your face to know that I loved you.
I would listen to your voice and I found that it soothed me.
When you were upset, I wanted to cry. But I did not have tears!
I could hear your laughter and if I would have known how to laugh,
I would have laughed too.

The sound I was so very fond of was the beat of your heart.
The percussion echoed with pitch perfect rhythm.
It was so peaceful and relaxing.
Its replicating melody was the best part.

You provided me shelter from the world, and gave me a place to grow.
I could not see much in there but would hear your voice loud and clear.
Inside I would toss and turn, I would flip and flop.
You kept me nourished through a cord attached to your belly from below.

A very long time passed. In that water I swam.
Then the strangest things happened? My water was gone!
I heard your voice, it was clearer, I saw an image.
It said, "Yes, my baby, here I am!"

At first I was in shock. I did not understand.
I started to cry. Where am I? What is going on?
Who is this looking down at me?
You had my body on your arm and my head on your hand.

You placed me on your warm chest.
That is when I realized, I heard the distinct music in my ear.
I began to smile.
I fell asleep listening to the sound I loved the best.

The most unconditional love is the love that a newborn child
feels for its mother.
This love is so innocent, so sweet.
This love is so pure. So full of emotion.
For that one moment in time it is all about her.

Unconditional Love

Every child is worthy of unconditional love.
That means to love without exceptions;
To show love and support all the time,
not just on special occasions.

Say "I love you" with meaning,
Teach without criticizing.
Unconditional love is more than just caring;
It is emotions that parents are sharing.

Unconditional love is supportive and encourages.
Regardless of the circumstances.
It is guiding and approving.
It is setting limits and not enabling.

It is unrestrictive,
And it is never invasive.
Unconditional love liberates.
It demonstrates.

So, look directly into your child's eyes.
They will then realize,
The depth of your Unconditional Love.
This love they will be ready to receive.

Loving Blanket of Arms

I use you as my blanket, I am wrapped in your warm embrace.
You are now sheltering me from the cooling temperatures.
I cannot feel the crispness of the night's air.
We are side by side, I can feel your smile on my face.

How foolish I was to forget my sweater.
You warned me that it was getting colder.
Maybe I was not foolish after all.
Maybe it was my plan to bring us closer together.

Sometimes I feel we do not hold each other enough.
We both have very demanding jobs.
We are raising the kids and caring for the house.
So making time for each other can be very tough.

Shall we dismiss the stresses we have in life?
Hold me closer to you for a little while longer.
Embrace me with your blanket of arms.
Keep me warm because you love, not just because I am your wife.

Moving Forward!

When I heard the news today,
I said, am I going to continue living my life this way?
Or are there some things that are in need of a change?
I do not want things to seem strange!

One thing I know for sure,
My life plans suddenly took a detour.
I accept them not to be my plans after all.
I know they are God's, and I am not afraid to go when He does call.

I also know from this second forward,
I want the good times to be remembered.
 I will love you like there is no tomorrow.
I do not want us to feel regret or sorrow.

I do not know when it will be my last second,
I do not want you to feel abandoned.
I do not want you to feel sad or afraid.
I do not want your tears to cascade.

I want you to feel happiness
In the knowing that that I will be with Jesus.
I will still be here to watch over you.
I will still be here to help guide you.

I am sorry my body you won't be able to see.
I am sorry you won't be able to touch me.
I am sorry it was my time to go!
I have always loved you!
This is the most important message for you to know!

Dancing in the Mist

The sky is gloomy, there is no sun to be found.
The moisture hovers densely in the air.
There is a peaceful breeze present.
I begin to look around.

Rain is falling in the form of a mist.
It is just enough to make one damp.
I smile to the sky,
On my face the water sprays. I can't resist.

Everyone else begins to dart inside.
I stand there for a moment,
Almost like I am in a trance.
Then I feel my love take my hand in his with pride.

He puts his arms around me and we begin to sway.
We do not care that others have stopped to watch.
We continue to dance.
It felt like we could dance the day away.

Rainy Day Reflections

Have you ever taken the time
To listen to the falling rain's rhythm?
There is a specific rhythmic sound,
As the rain falls through the trees then softly falls to the ground.

Taking the time to hear, one will be able to notice the difference,
 In the cadences, each bringing a wonderful balance.
Watching this falling rain is very peaceful.
The experience can be something very special.

Some might even be able to use this to meditate.
However, one must be able to deeply appreciate,
There are no specific words to explain,
The beauty of the falling rain.

True Love is described as the same.
With balance and peace, one can passionately proclaim.
The tenderness, the cadence.
So, when the rhythm of love is present, feel it with silence.

In the Glow of the Flame

On a chilly night,
We sat by a bonfire.
My love's face illuminated in the glow of the light.
We glanced at each other.

I noticed the beauty that was enhanced by the flame.
I reached my hand out to her.
I softly whispered her name.
I motioned for her to move closer.

She shifted closer to me.
She placed her head on my shoulder,
I rested my hand on her knee.
We noticed that the night was getting colder.

I got up and put another log on the fire,
As the flames again began to glow,
I looked deep into her eyes. I told her how much I loved her.
My love is stronger than yesterday, but will be even stronger tomorrow.

Name on a Tree

I was out shopping one day when I passed an angel tree.
I stopped and looked at that tree for a while.
I looked for the name that spoke to me.
When I found the right one, I started to smile.

I knew that because of me,
I could give something to someone in need.
At least one Christmas item would be a guarantee.
After all this is a time of giving and not of greed.

It hurts my heart to see any child do without.
I proceeded to shop. I could buy everything. I could go wild!
Instead I picked the perfect gift, then I checked out.

I knew I would not ever meet the receiver of this present.
None of that even mattered.
Just knowing that I could make someone happy, even if just for a moment.
I bought a gift that was sure to be remembered.

RIVER BANK ENCOUNTER

I laid down on the river's bank.
I just needed somewhere quiet, somewhere I could just think.
My chin propped in my hands.
I was there reflecting about Life's stressful demands.

Out of the corner of my eye,
I saw a shadow sit down nearby.
I sat up, to get a better look.
A man was staring, like I was a picture in a book.

He said nothing for a long while,
Yet I could not help but to smile.
I could sense the love in his eyes.
Somehow I knew this was a man of truth and no lies.

Finally, the silence was broken.
I hope you are not startled, by me sitting here unspoken.
It is just that your beauty left me speechless.
You are just like a Mona Lisa on a live canvas.

Dose of Reality

I am sorry my dear, I am running late.
I have to be to work by eight.
As I am blowing a kiss through the door.
Maybe tomorrow we can make a date.

No time for a loving embrace.
Not taking the time to stop and care.
How this might make her feel, because
We are living in a world that is a full throttle race.

On my drive into the office, I reflect upon my actions.
I can see her face before me. I see the tears in her eyes.
I know how much I have hurt her, I vow from that day forward,
I would put those who l love before anything else that beckons.

Hearing the News of Cancer is like a Being Hit by a Natural Disaster

I felt that my world as I knew it had just crumbled.
My rock that was once solid and strong was now fragile and weakened.
My insides would not stop trembling. I cannot prevent the shaking.
I tried to push forward but I stumbled.

Each day I see the damage and the destruction.
When I first heard the devastating news.
It was so overwhelming, I was in disbelief.
My heart was flooded with emotions never felt before.

I glanced around to see if anyone else felt the impact of my shock.
The force of the jolt, knocked all breath from me.
I felt like I just got smacked in the face by a tornado.
My eyes produced tears like hurricane rains.
I whispered, "Please turn back the clock."

Not Just A Day at the Beach

The water was a mix of Emerald and Jade.
On the shoreline the little children played.
Their laughter vibrated off the waves,
They ran, jumped, splashed, and did hand waves.

They did not care that the fish nibbled their toes,
Or that the hot sun beamed down on their nose.
There were no complaints about the taste of salt upon their lips.
It was day all about family and they even made new friendships.

At one point they were all hand and hand,
As they helped each other back on to the sand.
All the children were eager to see the blue crab;
Not one of them minded that it had claws, that could pinch and grab.

The proud parents watched from afar with love in their eyes,
Underneath the aqua blue skies.
They took pictures of their children and their beach scenes,
To keep for their memories.

Mama, it is Your Love and Strength

Mama, I thought I would be okay.
I thought I would be prepared.
I did all I could do to get ready.
For today.

But Mama, I lied.
I thought I was strong like you.
I love you so much.
I am sorry I cried.

I am glad you are not suffering any more.
It hurt just as bad to see that pain in your eyes.
Don't worry about me, I will be fine.
You have a beautiful dwelling to explore.

God has called you home to be free.
It is your love and strength,
That will get me through my own pain.
I now have the best of the angels with me.

THE PERFECT ROSES TAKE TIME

He had been right on time for thirty years,
Tonight she could not contain the tears.
She thought, Where is he?
Why is he so late? Where could he be?

Her thoughts went crazy. Has he been in a wreck?
Frantically she called the hospital, she just had to check!
No one had been brought in with his name.
She knew she could not be without him. Life would not be the same.

She called the bank to see if she had enough money for bail,
Just in case he was in jail.
She noticed money was missing from their account.
She was not certain of the exact amount.

She started thinking, Does he not love her anymore; does he not care?
Is he having an affair?
Several hours later, she heard his car.
Then the door opened but not very far.

He handed her a bouquet of roses; that were so perfect, so beautiful, and so red.
"Happy Anniversary! I Love You!" her husband said.
He got out of the car, and then, "I am sorry I am so late.
It took longer than I thought to find the perfect roses,
for the love of my life on this very special date."

Falling in Love

The day one finds love – it will not be the day you meet.
It will not be the day you marry.
It will be the day when the physical features no longer matter.
It will be the day when the joyously goes away.
It will be the day they turn to you and say, "When was that?"
It will be the day when they are no longer able to stand from age.
It will be the day that you can take care of someone when they
are medically fragile.
It will be the day when you say … good-bye.

Your Love Leads My Soul

Your love leads my soul.
Your love lets me know what to do.
On the days when I don't know where to go,
I come to you. Take my heart with you as you stroll.

Baby, I can't make it without you!
I want to you know,
Just how much it is that I need you too.
In my arms, close to me, I hold you.

Your love guides my every emotion.
I surrender to you my complete devotion.
Your love is my inspiration.
Your love is my motivation.

Good morning

It is such a beautiful morning.
I stepped out as I always do.
The bird flew by just to say hi.
He or she could have flied right on by,
but choose to stop and make my day with good morning chirps.
I did not see what kind of bird it was.
For that matter, I did not need to the lovely sound was enough.
Now I can get on with my day as it flew away.

LETTER FROM HEAVEN, I LOVE YOU, MOM

Mom, I hope by now you understand,
"That it's Okay," I am in the Promised Land
He told me that one day I would "Fly Away."
My Father said, "I am coming for you one day."

He said, "Fly with me, my Child." I said, "Father, I am ready!"
He did not take my life; He gave me eternity.
I am with our Heavenly Father.
Where I can play and hold the hand of your mother.

Mom, there are so many flowers! I will save the prettiest one for you.
You have to wait, because it is not your time though,
        you still have more to do.
When it is your time, I will run to you with all of my charms.
I will receive you with smiles and open arms.

I will watch over you as you have always done for me.
I am your protector now you see.
Father said I did a good job by helping so many.
Love always, your Buddy.

The Healing Bridge

I am healing. I am crossing the bridge from the darkness.
I am regaining control of my life. I am discovering who I am.
I know what I have done. I am learning I can no longer blame you.
I am yearning to live, love and to deal again.
I am not worthless!

We all have done our share of wrong deeds.
I can only be accountable for my own actions,
I have to learn to forgive others for their actions;
For these actions, that I now know were not of my control.
I have to try and make amends and see where the road leads.

My accountability starts with self-forgiving.
Let me just say, this is not an easy task!
I have been quite sinister. I have not been a saint!
There are still days where I still feel that, who am I kidding!

I can slowly feel the warmth of the love from inside my heart.
It is starting to pump through my frosty veins.
It is validating the hidden self-worth.
That is helping me make this fresh new healing start.

I am hoping that with this new eternal love that I am feeling,
I will be able to one day to project out, of my beating heart,
towards others that have hurt me.
This will truly give me a complete sense of healing.

Rainbows and Sunshine

Remember, storms never last
Don't make thunder if the sky is just overcast.
Start each day as a new day.
Let love lead the way.

Take a breath and look to the sky,
Wipe the tears from your eye.
You can still feel the warmth of the sunshine.
Please know that are hearts still intertwine

Even though you feel as though your skies are nothing but gray,
They are not here to stay.
Find the rainbow.
Know that I do love you so.

Sometimes you must walk through the stormy waters,
To appreciate all the beautiful colors.
Sometimes the heat of the sun rises,
Then through it all, the love surges.

Is The Love Captured Deep Within the Heart

As the old saying goes: Time heals all pains!
I am not sure this is entirely true.
As the days, months and years go by, the pain lessens.
How can one completely heal when the love remains?

When the love was so strong, how does time allow one to heal?
On certain days one will experience the effects of the pain all over again,
Just as it happened that very day.
The days may be filled with such emotion that it may be hard to deal.

The ones left behind will consistently think of the love lost.
They will yearn for it. They will cry for it.
They will tell others about it, and they will continue to love,
Until their very own breath has become lost.

The physical presence gone long ago, the memories remain.
The love captured deep within the heart.
Time has come and passed.
Still particular times, there is so much pain.

IT IS IN THE EYES

I when I look into your eyes, I still see their lovely sparkle.
They glisten like diamonds.
I love the way they lift me out of the darkest of moods.
They remind me of the stars the way they twinkle.

They can definitely hold my attention.
If I look into your eyes for too long I will get lost.
My mind will start to ponder.
I then have to look away because of the thoughts that I envision.

This still happens to me even after all of these years.
The reaction is the same on happy and sad days.
I have to be honest.
It hurts my heart to see them moistened with tears.

When it gets to be too much and I can no longer hold your stare,
I will turn my head or glance away.
You now will know why!
It is because my mind was hypnotized – by your beautiful pair.

I will Listen

You cry. I will listen,
I will come to you.
I will hold you. I will support you,
As you release your inner emotion.

When you want to talk, I will listen.
I can never get tired of your words.
Even if your speech is endless,
And you repeat the same question.

You sing. I will listen
To me your voice is a soothing instrument.
It does not matter if you are in pitch or you hit every note.
As a mother who loves her child, I do not look for imperfection.

You laugh. I will listen.
For this sound fills my heart with happiness.
Your love and laughter is the best kind of medication.

STRENGTH

There are many days when I feel the world's weight.
I feel as if I have this emotion. I do not know how to communicate.
I feel like all this burden is crashing down on me.
I feel like my mind and my heart are going to collapse emotionally.

He comes and sits down at my side.
At first I do not notice, I am usually preoccupied.
He starts holding my hand,
He says to me, "Please help me to understand."

Tell me what it is that you are going through?
So that I know how to better help you."
He places his arm around me, so tenderly.
He says, "I will hold you up when you are unsteady."

He says, "Go on now, my dear, it is okay to cry."
As he wipes the moisture so softly from my eye.
"True love will never judge,
Even if you want to sit here forever and never budge."

Slowly my head begins to rise;
As he smiles at me through those emerald eyes.
Once again he takes my hand;
He gently pulls me to my feet to stand.

He is always so compassionate and so dedicated.
I knew from that day; his love was the strength that I needed.
He knows just how to encourage my spirit to ascend.
He will always be my foundation, my best friend.

Star Gazing at Midnight with My Love

We go out to the beach just before twilight.
The sun is descending for the day.
We lay our blankets down upon the golden sand.
We sit watching the people packing up, leaving for the night.

We both lay down on our blanket, we talk for a while.
The sky above us continues to get darker and darker.
Yet it is ever so clear.
One by one they begin to appear. We both begin to smile.

We listen to the sounds of the waves as they come into the shores.
It is so peaceful out here, with all of this nature.
We both agree that laying here
Is much better than being somewhere indoors.

Star gazing with my love at midnight,
On a quiet peaceful beach,
Surrounded by nature,
Surely is a wonderful delight.

ALSO FROM ENERGION PUBLICATIONS

Noise Flash

a collection of poems about people, places, & things

By Lee Baker

...an from torrence. ...ds how to
...11 how to solve how to better everyone everything
thank you torrence come and save us all from killing
ourselves drowning our dreams with thoughts

"I really enjoyed the process of writing this book and writing is always cheaper than counseling," says Lee Baker. "It's a good outlet for crazy people. In my life, crazy is in abundant supply."

ALSO BY TABITHA EDWARDS-WALTON

Just $9.99 direct from Energion Publications or available via on-line retailers.

Poetic Life Experiences

Tabitha Edwards-Walton

More from Energion Publications

Personal Study

Finding My Way in Christianity	Herold Weiss	$16.99
The Jesus Paradigm	David Alan Black	$17.99

Christian Living

Faith in the Public Square	Robert D. Cornwall	$16.99
Grief: Finding the Candle of Light	Jody Neufeld	$8.99
Surviving a Son's Suicide	Ron Higdon	$9.99
If Your Child Is Gay	Steve Kindle	$9.99

Bible Study

Learning and Living Scripture	Lentz/Neufeld	$12.99
When People Speak for God	Henry Neufeld	$17.99
Luke: A Participatory Study Guide	Geoffrey Lentz	$8.99
Philippians: A Participatory Study Guide	Bruce Epperly	$9.99
Ephesians: A Participatory Study Guide	Robert D. Cornwall	$9.99
Evidence for the Bible	Elgin Hushbeck, Jr.	

Theology

Creation in Scripture	Herold Weiss	$12.99
Creation: the Christian Doctrine	Edward W. H. Vick	$12.99
Creation in Contemporary Experience	David Moffett-Moore	$9.99
Ultimate Allegiance	Robert D. Cornwall	$9.99
Reframing a Relevant Faith	Drew Smith	$11.99
The Journey to the Undiscovered Country	William Powell Tuck	$9.99
The River of LIfe	Lee Harmon	$9.99
Process Theology	Bruce Epperly	$4.99

Ministry

Clergy Table Talk	Kent Ira Groff	$9.99
So Much Older Then ...	Robert LaRochelle	$9.99
The Caregiver's Beatitudes	Robert Martin	$4.99
The Vicar of Tent Town	Shauna Hyde	$9.99

Generous Quantity Discounts Available
Dealer Inquiries Welcome
Energion Publications — P.O. Box 841
Gonzalez, FL 32560
Website: http://energionpubs.com
Phone: (850) 525-3916

www.ingramcontent.com/pod-product-compliance
Lightning Source LLC
Chambersburg PA
CBHW031617040426
42452CB00006B/570